"Reflections -
for living life fully."

... all thoughts are originals of :~

...Brock Tully

illustrations :~

...Heidi Thompson

calligraphy :~

...Brock Tully

Introduction...

"... to me, life is simple,
            'we've' made it complicated,
    & the challenge is
            to get back in touch
                    with it's simplicity..."

... i hope, through this little book, you
    are able to see more clearly why 'we'
    lose touch with our hearts, & how
    we 'can' & need to regain this closeness
    if we are to experience 'peace within
    towards a more peaceful world.'

Dedicated to ...

... the child, i believe, is 'within' us all ! i especially want to thank 'mine', who wouldn't allow me to 'numb' myself any longer, ; while i was doing a 10,000 mile bicycle journey, he opened me up to my heart's inner voice ; i knew ...

"... i'd rather be seen
for who i am
; be alone,
than be accepted
for someone i'm not
; be lonely."

"... i used to 'think'
                    so hard
        about how i thought
                    i should be ...

    now i 'am'
                    so easily
        who i can be."

"... some people
          love to be intelligent,
but they're not
          necessarily wise---

a wise person
          appreciates their intelligence,
but knows what's necessary
          is their love."

"--- i'm not wondering
                    where i'm going,
          after i die---

     i'm going after
                    the wonders of living,
          while i'm alive."

"... i want to have children
            because i love them,
¦ i want to love them
            once i have them...

¦ i want to keep loving
            `the child` in them
      even after i can't keep them
            as children."

"... it's not so important
                to think about
        the things
                i don't have,
                ¿ how to get them ...
as it is to appreciate
                        the things
        i do have,
                ¿ Why it's important
                not to forget them."

"... when i work at something
               i don't like
         because i think i need
                   lots of money,
   i seem to need more money
                   to do things
         i think will make me happy,
   & i need to spend
                   even more money
         on ways to get 'high'
                   doing them ---
when i do what i love,
         i seem to love being high'
               on the simple things in life,
         & i don't need much money
                   to do them."

"--- as i'm getting older,
    i'm seeing that
            how wise i am,
        isn't,
            how old i am,
        but,
            how 'here' i am."

"... When i'm confused ---

--- it's better
        to say what i'm feeling,
    ¿ have it sound confusing
                to someone ---

than to confuse someone
        by waiting
    until i can say it,
            better."

"--- when i'm wise
       i see that, often,
            my anger isn't with others...

         it's from my expectations
                        of others,
              to be otherwise."

"... when i was unhappy,
      i remembered what
           i wanted to forget,
    ¦ i forgot what
           i needed to remember ---

as i'm becoming happier,
      i'm remembering
        i can learn
    from what i thought
          i wanted to forget,
    ¦ i'm not forgetting
              to remember
      what used to be
           forgotten."

"... success is not
   what i do,
         & what others think
   about it ...
   success is
      how i do it,
         & that i feel good in my heart
   about it."

"... i never want to give
'an opportunity'
the chance
to slip by...

... it may
never give me
a second chance."

"... When i 'worry' about someone ---
i'm not believing in them,
i'm only giving myself power,
& they become weaker...

When i 'care' about someone...
i'm believing in them,
& i'm giving them extra strength
to become stronger."

"... when we're sensitive
            we can believe
            we're not strong ...

or we can feel strong
            by 'believing in'
    our sensitivity."

"... a big mistake, for me,
    is being afraid
                of making mistakes...
when i make this mistake,
    i make an even
             bigger mistake
of being critical & unforgiving
      of those
          who make mistakes,
& i don't see...

... the beautiful thing
      about making a mistake
  is that it is no longer
            a mistake
if we learn from it."

" ... a great strength

is being gentle

with our weaknesses."

"... either,

    we are all strangers,

        as i've lived with me

                all my life

    & i don't even know

        who i am yet ...

  or,

    none of us are strangers,

        if we see the beautiful 'essence'

              within everyone...

    ... it's that 'essence'

        that we, too often, have

           become strangers with."

"... When we're children,
        We have
            limitless imaginations ...

When we grow up,
            We are often limited
        by our image."

" ... 'intelligence' is
              what we know...
       'wisdom' is
              what we do
                     with what we know...
       'awareness' is
              knowing why we do
              what we do
                     with what we know...

       'happiness' is
              doing it."

"... i want to wish you a
        "Happy Birthday",
 & let you know
            that since your birth
 my days have been happier."

~ Love ~

"... When i want to get most
                    from others,
        i usually feel i have the least to give...

When i start giving to others
                    what i'm wanting,
        i stop wanting to get,
            because i see that i get
                            what i want,
                by giving."

"... even though
       you're in my presence,
                too little...

       you're in my thoughts,
                a lot
       & you're in my heart,
                always."

"--- sometimes i live
in my 'head',
sometimes i live
in my 'heart'...
but,
i know i'll get
'ahead'
if i have
the 'guts'
to follow
my 'heart'
& become
a 'liver'. ☺

"... when i go from A to B,
            it's not so important
      that i get to B,
   or what i get 'to be'
   for getting to B,
but that i don't forget
                  about 'being',
      while i'm going
            from A to B."

or,

      "... i'd rather
                  be 'growing'...
      than to be grown,
            & stop 'being'."

"... i don't want to be
        motivated by my anger,
                at the way things are,
    'just'
        at the moment
            something upsets me ---

i want to be motivated
            at every moment,
    so that i can do something,
        about the things
                that upset me,
            before they happen."

* inspired by Martin Luther King.

"... it's important
        to love to have goals
              that i can see...
but,
    my main goal
        is to see
              that i 'love'."

"... i'm not excited
            about the challenge
of winning
            someone else's heart,
so i'll feel good
            for a little while...

i am excited
            about the challenge
of staying in touch
            with my own heart,
so i'll know 'how'
            to feel good forever."

"... my body
            has an age...
my mind
            isn't aging...
¿ my heart
            is ageless."

"--- if i don't live
          in the 'now,'
     because i'm worried
          about my future,
then in the future,
     i'll probably be worried about
          my future's future ---

if i live in the 'now,'
          now,
     i'll probably be living
          in the 'now,'
               in the future,
& i'll see there was nothing
          to worry about,
               before."

"... i don't want
            to fail ...

... but i'd rather
            take a risk
    ¿ maybe fail ...
... than fail
            to take a risk,
    ¿ always wonder,
            'maybe if'..."

"--- when i worry
    'too much' about
                how i look,
    i seem to attract
        'too many' who only care
                about my looks,
    & it makes me wonder
                if anyone cares---
--- when i care more
        about how i feel,
    i may only attract a few
        who care about my feelings,
but,
    i'll get more of the feeling
        that people do care."

"... i want you
        to be happy
                to see me ---

but,
    i don't want you
        to need to see me
                for your happiness."

"... When i'm discouraged,
            i only have problems;
        i avoid or 'numb' pain;
            i feel miserable;
    & i don't know
            i'm dying ...

    ... when i start to grow,
        my problems become challenges,
            & even though i feel pain,
    it feels good to know
            i'm living."

"... i learn most from you,
        not when you
               'try' to teach me...
but,
    when you 'are',
        what you want me
            to know."

"... When we're children,
          we love to learn ...
too often,
     When we're grown-ups,
              we love to be right about
          What we think we've learned ...

          ; we love to teach those
                    who love to learn,
     but we forget to learn
              What those who love to learn
                    are teaching us !"

"--- i think
        'being on time'
is being thoughtful
        of another 'being's'
                time."

"... When i have a poor self-image,
i seem to attract people
who treat me like
i 'feel' i deserve,
& they seem to need to say
'i love you' more,
they show it less,
& yet they need me most ...

When i'm caring more about myself,
i seem to attract those
who treat me like
i 'know' i deserve,
& they seem to want to say
'i love you' more,
they need to say it less,
& yet they show it the most."

"... When i'm unhappy,
    i'm busy spending my time
        telling others
    What they should do...
When i'm busy doing
        what makes me happy,
    i don't have time
        to tell others
    What to do."

"When i'm happy with myself,
i'm not afraid
           that changes
will be scarey...

When i'm unhappy with myself,
i'm afraid
           of change,
& that's what's scarey."

"Love"

"... the blind can't see,
            how we who see,
    can be so blind
                to seeing,
    that what's most worthy
                of seeing,
    cannot be seen
                by the eye."

"... as i learn
    to listen to my heart,
        i'm learning more & more,
that i need to unlearn
    the fears
        i learned before."

"... what i get
        most from you,
    is not what you
        give to me...

    ... it's what i get
        from seeing
    how much you give
        to others."

" ... i'm sharing these thoughts
'with the hope'
that they touch you ...

...¦ to let you know
that i lose touch
too."

... to get any of Brock Tully's 'Reflections' books in your area ...

            bookstores ¿ gift stores can contact...
Green Tiger Press, Inc.
435 East Carmel St.
San Marcos, California,
   92069 ~ 4362
   (619) 744-7575
   1 (800) 424-2443 (outside California)...
or other Green Tiger distributors.

'a list of special books'

- books recommended in my first 'Reflections' book
- "Handbook to Higher Consciousness"- ken keyes
- "Hope for the Flowers"- Trina Paulus
- "Healing the Child Within"- Charles L. Whitfield
- everything by & about Gandhi & Martin Luther king
- "Good Dog, Carl"- Alexandra Day
- "Necessary Losses"- Judith Viorst
- "The Far Side"- Gary Larson
- anything by Leo Buscaglia
- "You Can Heal Your Life"- Louise L. Hay
- "Winnie-the-Pooh"- A.A. Milne
- "The Drama of the Gifted Child"- Alice Miller
- "The Giving Tree"- Shel Silverstein
- "The Terry Fox Story"- Canadian who ran across
                          Canada on one leg.
- "It Will Never Happen to Me"- Claudia Black
- lots of children's books!
- Jon-Lee kootnekoff- still hasn't written one! ☺